The Story of a Special Day
Volume 73

March 13

72nd day of the year
(73rd in leap years)
293 days remaining
until the end of the year.

by Michael Dobson

Timespinner
Press

For more information about the series, about me, or about your special day, please email us at editor@timespinnerpress.com.

Look for other volumes in *The Story of a Special Day*, coming often.

Table of Contents

Cover: The planet Uranus, discovered by Sir William Herschel on March 13, 1781.

Back Cover: The month of March, from the French Gothic illuminated manuscript *Les Très Riches Heures du duc de Berry.*

March 13 Quotations

"Living is a pretty grim joke, but a joke just the same."

— *L. Ron Hubbard, born March 13, 1911*

"That Mars is inhabited by beings of some sort or other we may consider as certain as it is uncertain what these beings may be."

— *Percival Lowell, born March 13, 1855*

"You can only protect your liberties in this world by protecting the other man's freedom. You can only be free if I am free."

— *Clarence Darrow, died March 13, 1938*

"Cautious, careful people, always casting about to preserve their reputation and social standing, never can bring about a reform. Those who are really in earnest must be willing to be anything or nothing in the world's estimation."

— *Susan B. Anthony, died March 13, 1906*

Event of the Day
The Discovery of Uranus

At the age of 19, William Herschel arrived in England, a refugee from the defeat of Hannover during the Seven Years' War. He was an oboist, after his father, who played in the Hannoverian Guard's military band, and also composed. While employed as a musician, he became interested in mathematics and lenses, leading to a new career building reflecting telescopes.

As an astronomer, Herschel began charting binary and multiple stars, creating three catalogues with over 800 observed entries. On March 13, 1781, he observed an oddity: the "star" had a disk, like a planet — but everyone knew there were only six planets! At first he classified his observation as a comet, but as the details of its orbit became clear, it was increasingly obvious that what Herschel had found wasn't a star or a comet, but a new planet. For the first time in history, the known boundaries of the Solar System had grown.

Herschel originally called the new planet the "Georgian star" after King George III, but the French called it "Herschel," because they weren't fond of the English king. Finally, the name "Uranus," for Greek deity known as the father of Zeus (Jupiter) and Cronus (Saturn), was chosen. However, the astronomical symbol for Uranus (♅) contains an "H" in honor of Herschel. In Chinese, Japanese, Korean, and Vietnamese, Uranus is "Sky King Star," or 天王星.

Although Uranus can be pronounced either *jʊərənəs* (with the emphasis on the first syllable) or *jʊ'reɪnəs* (with a long "a" sound and emphasis on the second), astronomers prefer the first pronunciation to avoid the grade school jokes.

Uranus, seventh planet from the Sun, is the fourth-largest planet, behind Jupiter, Saturn, and Neptune, and is about 14.5 times the mass of Earth. It is about 3 billion kilometers from the Sun, and its year is 84 times as long as ours.

Unlike the "gas giants" of Jupiter and Saturn, Uranus has more frozen water, ammonia, and methane, around a core of rock. For that reason, Uranus and Neptune are often called "ice giants." Uranus has the coldest atmosphere in the solar system, as low as -224° C (49° K). Like Saturn, Uranus has rings. It has 27 known moons, the largest being Titania and Oberon.

Unique among the planets, Uranus is tilted almost on its side. While day and night cycles near the equator are similar to other planets (about 17 hours in a day), at the poles the days are 42 years long followed by 42 years of total darkness.

It's possible (barely) to see Uranus with the naked eye, and fairly easy to see with binoculars or a small telescope. In fact, it had been spotted many times before Herschel, but had always been mistaken for a star.

Herschel's discovery of Uranus led to his appointment as the King's Astronomer. He continued to manufacture telescopes for leading astronomers throughout Europe, and searched for nebulae, eventually cataloguing over 2,400 objects. In observing the Sun, he also discovered infrared radiation.

Herschel's sister Caroline and son John also became noted astronomers in their own right. He received many honors, including a knighthood, and helped found the Royal Astronomical Society. The element uranium is named for the planet he discovered, and the Herschel Space Observatory, the largest space telescope, is named for him.

Herschel died in 1822 and is buried at St. Laurence's Church, Upton. The house where he first observed Uranus is now the Herschel Museum of Astronomy.

Portrait of Sir William Herschel by Lemuel Francis Abbott

March 13 Holidays and Celebrations

Kasuga Matsuri (Kasuga Grand Shrine, Nara, Japan)

 The Kasuga Grand Shrine (春日大社), one of the most beautiful and ancient in Japan, was built in 768 CE, and is registered as a UNESCO World Heritage Site. Each year on March 13, the Kasuga Matsuri, or "Monkey Festival" is held, with elaborate performances of ancient Imperial court music and ceremonial dances.

Christian Feast Days

Saints commemorated on March 13 include Euphrasia of Constantinople, Gerald of Mayo, Leander of Seville, Leticia, Nicephorus, Roderick, and Sabinus of Hermopolis.

What Happened on March 13?

624 CE - Battle of Badr (غزوة بدر)

The religion of Islam began in Mecca, but by 622, Muhammad and his early followers were forced to flee Mecca for nearby Medina in what is known as the *hijra* (وجْرَة). Hostilities between the Muslims of Medina and the Quraish of Mecca escalated, and on March 13, 624, a force of 300 Muslims commanded by Muhammad fought 900 Quraish at the wells of Badr, some 80 miles southwest of Medina. The Battle of Badr, one of the few specifically mentioned in the Quran (القرآن), ended in a decisive Muslim victory, a turning point in the fortunes of the young religion of Islam.

1591 CE - Battle of Tondibi

In 1590, the Sultanate of Morocco invaded the Songhai Empire of western Africa, one of the largest Islamic empires in history. In the Battle of Tondibi on March 13, 1591, some 4,500

Moroccan soldiers defeated a much larger force of over 22,000 Songhai in a decisive victory that ended the Songhai Empire as a regional power.

1697 CE - Spain Conquers Guatemala

After the Spanish conquest of Mexico, colonizers steadily moved south, coming into conflict with various Mesoamerican kingdoms, primarily Mayan. It took nearly two centuries for the Spanish forces to take control of what is now Guatemala, ending on March 13, 1697, when the Itza capital of Nojpetén fell.

1884 CE - Siege of Khartoum

On March 13, 1884, an Egyptian force commanded by British General Charles George Gordon was trapped in the Sudanese city of Khartoum by a force of 50,000 Sudanese led by Muhammad Ahmad, who had proclaimed himself to be the Mahdi (مهدي), a prophesied messiah of Islam. The siege lasted ten months before the Mahdists broke into the city and killed the entire garrison on the night of January 25-26, 1885.

"Death of General Gordon at Khartoum," by J. L. G. Ferris

1920 CE - Kapp-Lüttwitz Putsch

On March 13, 1920, a coup led by Wolfgang Kapp and Walther von Lüttwitz tried to overthrow Germany's Weimar Republic and establish an authoritarian government. The revolutionaries occupied Berlin, but were defeated when the working class of Germany went on a general strike.

1940 CE - End of the Winter War

On March 13, 1940, the Moscow Peace Treaty betwen Finland and the Soviet Union went into effect, ending the Winter War between the two countries. Although the treaty ceded parts of Finland to the Soviet Union, it preserved Finland's independence.

1943 CE - Kraków Ghetto Liquidated

Beginning in 1941, the Nazis began forcing Jews in the Podgórize district of occupied Poland into the Kraków Ghetto. Waves of deportations transported thousands of ghetto residents into concentration camps. The final liquidation of the ghetto took place on March 13-14, 1943, when SS troops deported 8,000 Jews to a labor camp, killed 2,000 on the spot, and transported all rcmaining residents to Auschwitz.

Deportations from the Kraków Ghetto

1954 CE - Battle of Điện Biên Phủ

Beginning on March 13, 1954, and lasting until May 7, Việt Minh communist-nationalist forces surrounded and besieged French forces in the regional capital of Điện Biên Phủ. In spite of efforts to resupply the French garrison of some 10,000 troops, it was overrun after a two month siege. This led directly to the withdrawal of the French from the region and the division of Vietnam into Ho Chi Minh's Democratic Republic of (North) Vietnam and the State of (South) Vietnam.

1964 CE - Murder of Kitty Genovese

On the night of March 13, 1964, New York City resident Kitty Genovese was stabbed to death near her home in the Kew Gardens section of Queens. This murder became a national story based on a New York *Times* article that began, "For more than half an hour thirty-eight respectable, law-abiding citizens in Queens watched a killer stalk and stab a woman in three separate attacks…" Later studies showed that the newspaper story, and its portrayal of callous city residents ignoring the screams of a helpless victim, was at best exaggerated and in many ways false. Nevertheless, research into the "bystander effect" shows that larger numbers of bystanders actually lowers the likelihood that someone will step forward to provide help.

1964 CE - Apollo 9 Returns

The third manned mission of the Apollo program launched on March 3, 1969, and splashed down in the North Atlantic on March 13. The mission was notable for the first docking, extraction, and manned flight of a Lunar Module, a key step on the path to the Moon.

Apollo 9 spacewalk

1985 CE - Kenilworth Road Riot

In one of the worst cases of football (soccer) hooliganism during the 1980s, a riot broke out during a match between Luton Town and Millwall at the Kenilworth Road stadium in Luton. Eighty-one people were injured, including 31 police, leading to Luton's expulsion and a ban on away supporters at Luton games.

1964 CE - Seikan Tunnel Opens

The Seikan Tunnel (青函トンネル), a 33-mile (54 kilometer) underwater railway tunnel in Japan that connects the main island of Honshu with Hokkaido. At its opening, it was both the longest and the deepest operational rail tunnel in the world.

1996 CE - Dunblane Massacre

On March 13, 1996, 43-year old Thomas Hamilton entered Dunblane Primary School in Scotland, carrying four handguns. He killed 16 children and one adult before committing suicide. As a result of the official inquiry, Britain passed new laws making private ownership of handguns illegal in the UK.

1997 CE - Lights Over Phoenix

On the night of March 13, 1997, several thousand people over a space of about 300 miles witnessed a triangular formation of lights followed by a series of stationary lights near Phoenix. At least some of the lights were flares dropped by A-10 Warthog aircraft on training exercises. Additional sightings took place in 2007 and 2008.

Who Was Born
on March 13?

The abbreviation "O.S." on some dates refers to the fact that the Russian Empire did not switch from the Julian to the Gregorian calendar at the same time as the rest of Europe, and therefore some figures have two dates for their birth or death.

People whose original names are not in the Western alphabet have their native names in the appropriate script shown in parenthesis.

Acting

Harry Melling (March 13, 1989 —)

Harry Melling played Dudley Dursley in the *Harry Potter* films.

Emile Hirsch (March 13, 1985 —)

Emile Hirsch starred in *Speed Racer* and *Milk*, and appeared in featured roles in *Lords of Dogtown, The Girl Next Door*, and other films.

Noel Fisher (March 13, 1984 —)

Noel Fisher played the school bully in *Max Keeble's Big Move* and starred in the miniseries *The Pacific* as Private Hamm in the battle of Okinawa.

April Matson (March 13, 1981 —)

April Matson is best known for playing Lori Trager on the ABC series *Kyle XY.*

Molly Stanton (March 13, 1980 —)

Molly Stanton played Charity Standish and her evil doppleganger on the soap opera *Passions.*

Danny Masterson (March 13, 1976 —)

Danny Masterson played Hyde in *That '70s Show.*

Chris Ashworth (March 13, 1975 —)

Chris Ashworth played Sergei Malatov on *The Wire.*

Tracy Wells (March 13, 1971 —)

Tracy Wells, also known as Tracy Tofte, is best known for playing Heather on the ABC sitcom *Mr. Belvedere*, winning a Young Artist Award.

Annabeth Gish (March 13, 1971 —)

Annabeth Gish played Monica Reyes on *The X-Files*, Elizabeth Bartlet Westin on *The West Wing,* and had a role in the movie *Mystic Pizza.*

Christopher Collet (March 13, 1968 —)

Christopher Collet had a lead role in the 1986 film *The Manhattan Project.*

Dana Delany (March 13, 1956 —)

Dana Delany won two Emmys for her role on the TV show *China Beach* and is also known for her starring role on the show *Body of Proof.*

Glenne Headly (March 13, 1955 —)

Actress Glenne Headly's first major role was in 1988's *Dirty Rotten Scoundrels*, following which she played Tess Trueheart in Warren Beatty's *Dick Tracy.*

Robin Duke (March 13, 1954 —)

Robin Duke was part of the cast of *Saturday Night Live* from 1981 to 1984.

Deborah Raffin (March 13, 1953 — November 21, 2012)

Deborah Raffin was nominated for a Golden Globe for her role in 1981's *Touched by Love*. She had a starring role in *Noble House* with Pierce Brosnan and appeared in the television series *7th Heaven* and *The Secret Life of the American Teenager*.

William H. Macy (March 13, 1950 —)

Macy was nominated for an Academy Award for his role in *Fargo*, and has also won two Emmys, along with numerous nominations.

Robert S. Woods (March 13, 1948 —)

Robert S. Woods won a Daytime Emmy for playing Bo Buchanan on the soap opera *One Life to Live*.

Leslie Parrish (March 13, 1935 —)

Leslie Parrish played Daisy Mae in 1959's *Li'l Abner* and the doomed Jocelyn Jordan in 1962's *The Manchurian Candidate*.

Joseph Mascolo (March 13, 1929 —)

Mascolo played Stefano DiMera in the soap opera *Days of Our Lives*.

Peter Breck (March 13, 1929 — February 6, 2012)

Peter Breck played middle son Nick in the 1960s Western *The Big Valley*.

Peter Breck (left) with Anna Lisa from *Black Saddle*

Art

Al Jaffee (March 13, 1921 —)

Cartoonist Al Jaffee is best known for his *Mad* Magazine work, including the legendary "fold-ins."

Business

Jamie Dimon (March 13, 1956 —)

Jamie Dimon is CEO of JPMorgan Chase. He was on *Time* Magazine's list of the world's 100 most influential people four times and was named CEO of the Year in 2011.

Military

Butch O'Hare (March 13, 1914 — November 26, 1943)

Edward "Butch" O'Hare was the first U.S. Navy ace and Medal of Honor winner in World War II. Chicago's O'Hare Airport is named for him.

Lt. Butch O'Hare in his Grumman F4F Wildcat

Albert William Stevens (March 13, 1886 — March 26, 1949)

U.S. Army Air Corps officer Albert Stevens took the first photograph of the Earth showing the curvature of the horizon, the first photograph of the Moon's shadow projected onto the Earth during an eclipse, and set a record for balloon ascent of nearly 14 miles in *Explorer II* (below).

Music and Dance

Common (March 13, 1972 —)

Lonnie Rashid Lynn, Jr., is an American rapper and actor under the stage name Common. He won two Grammy Awards and has appeared in numerous films including *Date Night* and *Street Kings*.

Adam Clayton (March 13, 1960 —)

Adam Clayton is best known as the bassist of the Irish band U2.

Scatman John (March 13, 1942 — December 3, 1999)

John Paul Larkin, better known by his stage name, is remembered for his 1995 hit "Scatman (Ski-Ba-Bop-Ba-Dop-Bop)."

Candi Staton (March 13, 1940 —)

Soul and gospel singer Candi Staton is known for her 1976 disco hit "Young Hearts Run Free," and is a member of the Christian Music Hall of Fame.

Christopher Gable (March 13, 1940 — October 23, 1998)

Choreographer and ballet dancer Christopher Gable was named a Commander of the Order of the British Empire for his services to British dance. In addition to his numerous stage roles, he had a role in a 1984 *Doctor Who* serial and appeared in several movies.

Neil Sedaka (March 13, 1939 —)

Neil Sedaka's pop hits include "Calendar Girl," "Happy Birthday Sweet Sixteen," and "Breaking Up Is Hard To Do."

Neil Sedaka

Mike Stoller (March 13, 1933 —)

Stoller and his long-time collaborator Jerry Leiber wrote "Hound Dog, "Jailhouse Rock," "Stand By Me," "On Broadway," and other hits.

Jan Howard (March 13, 1930 —)

Grand Ole Opry star Jan Howard is best known for her 1966 country hit "Evil on Your Mind" and her 1967 duet with Bill Anderson, "For Loving You."

Roy Haynes (March 13, 1925 —)

Jazz drummer and bandleader Roy Haynes was part of Charlie Parker's quintet and worked with Stan Getz and Sarah Vaughan. He received a Grammy Lifetime Achievement Award in 2010.

Sammy Kaye (March 13, 1910 — June 2, 1987)

Big Band era bandleader Sammy Kaye was famous for his tag line, "Swing and sway with Sammy Kaye."

Newsmakers

Daniel Lambert (March 13, 1770 — June 21, 1809)

Jailkeeper and animal breeder Daniel Lambert was famous for being the heaviest authenticated person in history up to his death. He weighed 50 stone, or 700 lbs. His poverty forced him to put himself on exhibition to raise money.

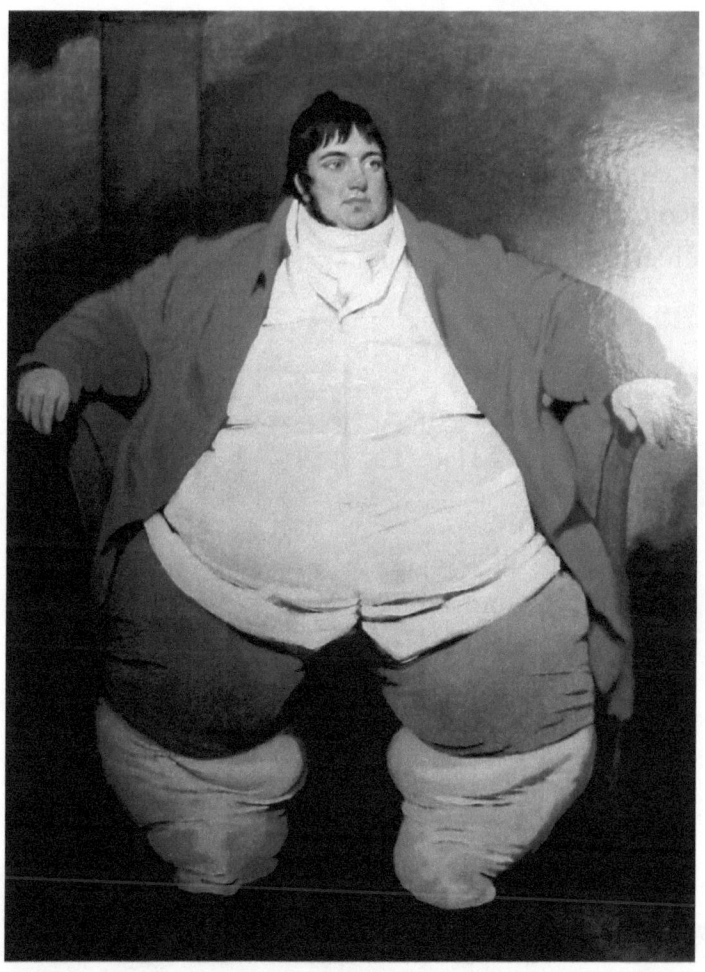

Portrait of Daniel Lambert by Benjamin Marshall

Politics and Government

William J. Casey (March 13, 1913 — May 6, 1987)

Casey was Director of Central Intelligence (DCI) from 1981 to 1987, responsible for overseeing the entire U.S. intelligence community. He was Ronald Reagan's campaign manager in the 1980 election.

Abigail Fillmore (March 13, 1798—March 30, 1853)

Abigail Fillmore, wife of President Millard Fillmore, was First Lady of the United States from 1850 to 1853.

Abigail Fillmore

Earl Grey (March 13, 1764— July 17, 1845)

Charles Grey, 2nd Earl Grey, was prime minister of the United Kingdom from 1830 to 1834. In addition to his political achievements, he is the namesake of Earl Grey tea.

Religion

L. Ron Hubbard (March 13, 1911 — January 24, 1986)

L. Ron Hubbard, originally known as an author of pulp science fiction and fantasy, founded the Church of Scientology.

Magazine cover featuring a story by L. Ron Hubbard

Science

Donella Meadows (March 13, 1941 — February 20, 2001)

Environmental scientist Donella Meadows is best known as lead author of the 1972 book *The Limits to Growth*.

John Hasbrouck Van Vleck (March 13, 1889 — October 27, 1980)

Van Vleck co-won the 1977 Nobel Prize in Physics for his contributions to understanding the behavior of electrons in magnetic solids.

Percival Lowell (March 13, 1855 — November 12, 1916)

Astronomer Percival Lowell is best known today for his speculation that there might be canals on the planet Mars, a belief that has since been discredited. A highly respected astronomer, he founded the Lowell Observatory and started the effort that led to the discovery of Pluto 14 years after his death. The choice of the name Pluto and its symbol, a stylized "PL," were both influenced by his initials: PL.

Joseph Priestley (March 13, 1733 [O.S.] — February 6, 1804)

Theologian, chemist, philosopher, and political theorist Joseph Priestley authored over 150 works in his lifetime. He is often credited as the discoverer of oxygen, though there are other claimants. He is also one of the inventors of soda water. His political opinions as one of the developers of utilitarianism got him into trouble later in life, and he fled to the United States, where he spent his remaining years.

John Theophilus Desaguiliers (March 13, 1683— February 29, 1744)

French-born British natural philosopher John Desaguliers won the Copley Medal of the Royal Society of London for his discoveries of the properties of electricity. He is credited as the inventor of the planetarium.

Sports

Marco Andretti (March 13, 1987 —)

Marco Andretti is an American auto racer who is part of the third generation of the famous Andretti racing family.

Caron Butler (March 13, 1980 —)

NBA forward Caron Butler started for the US team that took the gold medal in the 2001 FIBA World Championship, and was Big East Player of the Year in 2002.

Johan Santana (March 13, 1979 —)

MLB starting pitcher Johan Santana is a two-time Cy Young Award winner and in 2012 threw the first no-hitter in New York Mets franchise history against the St. Louis Cardinals.

Andrés Escobar (March 13, 1967 — July 2, 1994)

Known as the "Gentleman of Football," soccer star Andrés Escobar was shot and killed in Medellín, Columbia, for his goal in the 1994 FIFA World Cup that resulted in gambling losses to several powerful drug lords.

Will Clark (March 13, 1964 —)

"Will the Thrill" Clark earned two Gold Glove, two Silver Slugger, and a Golden Spike Award, as well as played on the silver medal-winning 1984 Summer Olympic baseball team.

Home Run Baker (March 13, 1886 — June 28, 1963)

John Franklin Baker was elected to the Baseball Hall of Fame in 1955. He is generally regarded as the best third baseman of the pre-war era.

Frank "Home Run" Baker

Writing and Publishing

Ridley Pearson (March 13, 1953 —)

Novelist Ridley Pearson has written New York *Times* best-selling suspense novels as well as childrens' adventure books including several prequels to Peter Pan co-authored with humorist Dave Barry.

Charles Krauthammer (March 13, 1950 —)

Conservative columnist and Pulitzer Prize winner Charles Krauthammer contributes to several magazines, newspapers, and television news programs.

Walter Annenberg (March 13, 1908 — October 1, 2002)

Walter Anneberg created and published *TV Guide* and *Seventeen* Magazine, and owned the Philadelphia *Inquirer* and other publications. In later life, he was a well known philanthropist who donated over $2 billion, primarily for education and the arts.

Hugh Walpole (March 13, 1884 — June 1, 1941)

English novelist Sir Hugh Walpole published 36 novels and was a leading literary figure of his day, but his works have been neglected since his death.

Sir Hugh Walpole

Who Died on March 13?

Acting and Theater

Betsy Blair (December 11, 1923 — March 13, 2009)

Actress Betsy Blair, first wife of Gene Kelly, was blacklisted by the House Un-American Activities Committee, but came back with a starring role in the 1955 film *Marty*, for which she received an Academy Award nomination.

Peter Tomarken (December 7, 1942 — March 13, 2006)

Tomarken was the host of the game show *Press Your Luck*.

Maureen Stapleton (June 21, 1925 — March 13, 2006)

Actress Maureen Stapleton was nominated for an Academy Award for her debut performance in *Lonelyhearts*, received another nomination for *Airport*, and won for 1981's *Reds,* playing anarchist Emma Goldman. She was inducted into the American Theatre Hall of Fame in 1981.

Garson Kanin (November 24, 1912 — March 13, 1999)

Writer and director Garson Kanin is best known for his 1946 play *Born Yesterday*, which was adapted into a 1950 movie of the same name. He also directed the stage play of T*he Diary of Anne Frank*, and is in the Theater Hall of Fame.

Krzysztof Kieślowski (June 27, 1941 — March 13, 1996)

Influential Polish director Krzysztof Kieślowski won numerous international awards, and is listed as #2 on the British Film Institute list of the top ten directors of modern times.

John Holmes (August 8, 1944 — March 13, 1988)

John C. Holmes, also known as Johnny Wadd, appeared in over 2,000 porongraphic films, and was involved in the 1981 Wonderland murders. His life inspired two movies, *Boogie Nights* and *Wonderland*.

Richard Burbage (January 6, 1567 — March 13, 1619)

English actor and theater owner Richard Burbage starred in the first performances of many of

Shakespeare's plays, including *Hamlet, Othello, Richard III*, and *King Lear* as a member of Shakespeare's own theater company, the Lord Chamberlain's Men.

Richard Burbage

Art and Cartooning

Lee Falk (April 28, 1911 — March 13, 1999)

Lee Falk is best known for the popular comic strips *The Phantom* and *Mandrake the Magician*, and also directed some 300 plays, including 12 he wrote.

Panel from a 1948 installment of *The Phantom* comic strip

Bill Reid (January 12, 1920 — March 13, 1998)

Canadian artist Bill Reid's work is featured on the Canadian $20 bank note.

Military

Odette Hallowes (April 28, 1912 — March 13, 1995)

Odette Hallowes was sent into Nazi-occupied France to work with the underground. Betrayed by a double agent, tortured by the Gestapo, and sent to a concentration camp, she kept to her cover story, escaped death, and was the first woman to win the George Cross while still alive as a reward for her heroism.

Henry Shrapnel (June 3, 1761 — March 13, 1949)

British army officer and inventor Henry Shrapnel invented the "shrapnel shell," a hollow cannonball filled with shot that would burst in mid-air. The term "shrapnel," referring to fragmentation of artillery shells and other objects, comes from his name.

Politics and Law

Clarence Darrow (April 18, 1857 — March 13, 1938)

Legendary lawyer and civil libertarian Clarence Darrow (below)defended teenage killers Leopold and Loeb in their sensational 1924 trial, and famously defended John Scopes in the "Monkey Trial" over the teaching of the Theory of Evolution.

Clarence Darrow —

Susan B. Anthony (February 15, 1820 — March 13, 1906)

Pioneering feminist Susan B. Anthony (below) was a leader in the movement for women's suffrage in the United States and co-founded the first Women's Temperance Movement.

Benjamin Harrison (August 20, 1833 — March 13, 1901)

Benjamin Harrison was the 23rd President of the United States (1889-1893) and a grandson of 9th President William Henry Harrison.

Tsar Alexander II of Russian (Александр II Николаевич) (April 29 [O.S. April 17], 1818 — March 13 [O.S. March 1], 1884)

Tsar Alexander II is known as Alexander the Liberator for emancipating the serfs of Russia.

Science and Academics

Robert C. Baker (December 19, 1921 — March 13, 2006)

Inventor and professor Robert C. Baker invented the chicken nugget, for which he was elected to the Poultry Hall of Fame.

Encarnacion Alonza (March 23, 1895 — March 13, 2001)

Alonza was the first Filipino woman to earn a Ph.D., and was named National Scientist of the Philippines in 1985.

Hans von Ohain (December 14, 1911 — March 13, 1998)

German engineer Hans von Ohain is one of the inventors of jet propulsion, developing the engine that powered the Heinkel He 178, the first all-jet aircraft, in 1939.

Heinkel He 178 jet aircraft with Ohain engine

Bruno Bettelheim (August 28, 1903 — March 13, 1990)

Child psychologist Bruno Bettelheim was internationally recognized for his work on Freud, psychoanalysis, and emotionally disturbed children.

Vittorio Jano (April 22, 1891 — March 13, 1965)

Chief Engineer for Alfa Romeo and later a senior engineer for Ferrari, Vittorio Jano designed performance engines for Grand Prix racing. His Ferrari V6 and V8 designs and their descendents continue to be used today.

Corrado Gini (May 23, 1884 — March 13, 1965)

Statistician and sociologist Corrado Gini is best known as the developer of the Gini coefficient, a measure of the income inequality in a society.

Leland Stanford, Jr. (May 14, 1868 — March 13, 1884)

Leland Stanford, Jr., was the son of Governor Leland Stanford of California. Stanford University (technically Leland Stanford Junior University) is named for him.

Sports

Test (March 17, 1975 — March 13, 2009)

WWE wrestler Andrew Martin won the Intercontinental and European Championships and was a world tag team champion as well.

Leon Day (October 30, 1916 — March 13, 1995)

Negro League pitcher Leon Day was elected to the Baseball Hall of Fame in 1995.

Writing

Stephen Vincent Benét (July 22, 1898 — March 13, 1943)

Author Stephen Vincent Benét won a 1929 Pulitzer Prize for *John Brown's Body* and is also known for his short stories "The Devil and Daniel Webster" and "By the Waters of Babylon." One of his stories was adapted into the movie *Seven Brides for Seven Brothers*.

The month of March, from the illuminated manuscript *Les Très Riches Heures du duc de Berry*

March: The Third Month

In ancient Rome, March was the first month of the year. As the first month of spring, in the Mediterranean climate it marked the beginning of the military campaign season. That's why March (Martius) is named in honor of Mars, the Roman god of war.

Although the first month of the year was moved back to January sometime during the transition of Rome from a kingdom to a republic (historians differ), March was the first month of the year in Russia until the end of the 15th Century, and is the first month of the year in many other cultures and religions.

In the northern hemisphere, March 1 marks the beginning of meteorological spring. In the southern hemisphere, March is the equivalent of September, making southern hemisphere March the beginning of autumn.

March is one of the seven months that have 31 days in it. March starts on the same day of the week as November every year, and except for leap years starts on the same day as February.

March starts on the same day of the week as the previous June except for leap years, and in leap years starts on the same day as the previous September and December.

March in Other Cultures

In Finland, March is called *maaliskuu* (earthy month). In Ukraine, it's *березень* (birch tree). Other names for March include *Lentmonat* (Saxon), *Hyld-monath* (Angles), and *sušec* (Slovene).

March Symbols

Birthstones: Aquamarine and bloodstone, both representing courage.

Aquamarine

Birth Flowers: Daffodils

Daffodils in Bagatelle Park, Paris, France

March Events

Honorary months: Presidents, Congresses, and nations around the world issue proclamations recognizing particular months to honor certain causes. These events generally fall in March. (All US unless otherwise noted.)

- National Nutrition Month

- American Red Cross Month

- Women's History Month (celebrated in Canada during October)

- Irish-American Heritage Month

- Colorectal Cancer Awareness Month

- Fire Prevention Month (The Philippines)

"March Madness": (United States) The NCAA Men's Division I Basketball Championship, popularly known as "March Madness" or the "Big Dance," is a single-elimination tournament to establish the champion college basketball team.

Multi-day events: Some March events span multiple days.

- **Nineteen Day Fast:** (Bahá'í Faith) March 2 through March 20

- **Girl Scout Week:** (U.S.) The week that includes March 12, the date of the founding of the first chapter of the Girl Scouts of the USA in 1912. The earliest Girl Scout Week can start is March 6, and the latest it can end is March 18. The Sunday of Girl Scout Week is celebrated by some churches as Girl Scout Sunday or Girl Scout Sabbath.

Movable events: Some events change dates from year to year.

- **Commonwealth Day:** Commonwealth Day, formerly Empire Day, celebrates the establishment of the Commonwealth of Nations. There is a service in Westminster Abbey and a speech by England's monarch to the Commonwealth nations around the world. Commonwealth Day is held annually on the second Monday in March, which can fall between March 8 and March 14.

- **Canberra Day:** In the Australian Capital Territory, Canberra Day celebrates the official naming of Australia's capital city. It is also held annually on the second Monday in March.

- **Passion Sunday:** The fifth Sunday of the Christian season of Lent is known as Passion Sunday in various Protestant denominations and by some traditionalist Catholics. Sometimes, the sixth Sunday of Lent is also known as Passion Sunday, but it is more commonly known as Palm Sunday. Passion Sunday starts the two week Passiontide, which ends on Holy Saturday, the day before Easter, commemorating the day that Jesus's body was laid in the tomb. The fifth Sunday of Lent can occur as early as March 8, and as late as April 11.

March Zodiac Signs

From the perspective of someone on Earth, the Sun appears to move through the sky throughout the year, along a path astronomers call the ecliptic plane. The ecliptic plane is divided into twelve constellations, known as the zodiac, based on traditionally observed patterns of stars. On your birthday, you can't see your constellation, because it's part of the daytime sky.

The zodiac was first developed by Babylonian astronomers about 2,500 years ago. Because they were unaware that the Earth wobbles like a spinning top (a motion known as precession), they didn't make allowance for the fact that the Sun's path through the zodiac changes over time.

That means there are now two sets of dates for your birth sign. The tropical dates are the original Babylonian dates; the siderial dates tell you where the Sun actually appears as it moves along its annual path.

March 13 is in Pisces in tropical dates, and is in Aquarius in siderial.

Aquarius

Tropical January 20 to February 19

Siderial February 12 to March 14

Aquarius is one of the oldest recognized constellations, originally representing the Babylonian god Ea. In Latin, Aquarius means "water-carrier," represented in its symbol. In Greek mythology, Aquarius is sometimes associated with Deucalion, who survived a world-cleansing flood. In Chinese astronomy, it is known as the Black Tortoise of the North (北方玄武, Běi Fāng Xuán Wǔ).

In astrology, Aquarius is considered to be masculine and extroverted, and despite the name is an air sign. Aquarians are supposed to be philanthropical, inventive, and individualistic.

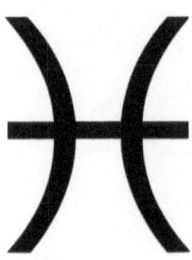

Pisces

Tropical February 20 to March 20

Siderial March 15 to April 14

In the Roman legend of Venus and her son Cupid, they escaped the clutches of Typhon, known as the "father of all monsters," by transforming into fish and tying themselves together with rope. That's why the name Pisces is plural for fish. The constellation appears as a somewhat ragged "V" shape, representing the rope, with the "fish" located at the two rope ends.

In astrology, Pisces is a water sign, compatible with the other water signs Cancer and Scorpio, as well as with the earth signs Taurus, Virgo, and Capricorn. Pisceans are supposed to be imaginative, compassionate, unworldly, secretive, and escapist.

What Day of the Week is March 13?

On what day of the week does March 13 fall?

Surprisingly, this isn't an easy question. Because the calendar year is 365 days long (366 in leap years), it doesn't divide evenly by the seven days of the week.

Also, the Earth goes around the Sun in about 365-1/4 days, so a calendar tends to drift over time. That's why the same date falls on different weekdays in different years.

This is made even more complicated by a change in calendars that took place in 1582. Our modern calendar has its roots in ancient Rome, in a calendar reform conducted by Julius Caesar. Caesar commissioned mathematicians to attack the problem, and came up with the idea of *leap years,* and thus standardized the calendar for centuries to come. This was called the *Julian calendar.*

Over time, however, the small errors in Caesar's calculation compounded. That's why Pope Gregory XIII commissioned the *Gregorian calendar,* used in most of the world today. Some countries converted in 1582, when the calendar was first developed; some converted later; other still haven't changed.

Gregorian and Julian aren't the only types of calendars. The Hebrew year, the Islamic year, and many other calendars are used in different parts of the world and among different people.

You can convert Gregorian dates to other calendars, including the Hebrew calendar, the Islamic calendar, and even the Mayan calendar by visiting the Fourmilab Calendar Converter at http://www.fourmilab.ch/documents/calendar/.

A 50-year brass perpetual calendar.

Copyright, Credit, and Contact

Follow Us

Our blog Dobson's Improbable History features short articles on events and people associated with each day, and updates several times each week. Get the latest on Twitter @SidewiseThinker.

Sources and Art Credits

All art and photographs are either in the public domain or used under a Creative Commons license. Attribution is provided where requested by the copyright owner or when of historical significance, listed below.

- The cover photograph of the planet Uranus is an infrared composite image was taken in 2004 by Lawrence Sromovsky at the W. M. Keck Observatory in Wisconsin as part of the NASA Solar System Exploration program. It is in the public domain as an image of NASA.

- The portrait of William Herschel was painted by Lemuel Francis Abbott in 1785, and is in the public domain because its copyright has expired. The original painting hangs in the National Portrait Gallery, London.

- The photograph of Kasuga-taisha, the Kasuga Grand Shrine, was taken by "663highland" and is used under the terms of the Creative Commons Attribution-Share Alike 3.0 Unported and the Creative Commons Attribution 2.5 Generic licenses.

- The print "Death of General Gordon at Khartoum" is by J. L. G. Ferris, first published around 1885. It is in the public domain because its copyright has expired.

- The photograph of Jews being deported from the Kraków Ghetto is from Istytut Pamieci Narodowej by way of the United States Holocaust Memorial Museum and is in the public domain in both Poland and the United States.

- The photograph from the Apollo 9 mission was taken by astronaut Russell L. Schweickart. It shows command module pilot David R. Scott during his EVA. It is in the public domain as an image of NASA.

- The photograph of Peter Breck and Anna Lisa from the TV series *Black Saddle* is in the public domain because it was published in the United States between 1923 and 1977 without a copyright notice.

- The cover for *Mad's Vastly Overrated Al Jaffee* is covered by copyright, but its use here is covered by U. S. fair use laws because it illustrates an educational article about the entity it represents, is used as the primary visual identification of the topic, is of low resolution and not suitable for the publication of counterfeit goods, is not used in such a way as to suggest to a reader that the use is authorized, and is not replaceable with an uncopyrighted image of comparable educational value.

- The photograph of Butch O'Hare is a work of the U. S. federal government and is thus in the public domain.

- The photograph of the Explorer II gondola in the National Air and Space Museum was taken by "Cliff" and is used under the Creative Commons Attribution 2.0 Generic license.

- The photograph of Neil Sedaka is by AVRO, and is from *Beeld En Geluid Wiki - Gallerie: Toppop 1974*. It is used here under the Creative Commons Attribution-Share Alike 3.0 Unported license.

- The 1806 portrait of Daniel Lambert by Benjamin Marshall is in the public domain because its copyright has expired.

- The official portrait photograph of Abigail Fillmore is a work of the U.S. federal government and thus in the public domain.

- The cover of *Fantastic Adventures* magazine, featuring a story by L. Ron Hubbard, is in the public domain because its copyright was not renewed.

- The photograph of Frank "Home Run" Baker is from the National Photo Collection at the Library of Congress. According to the Library, there are no known restriction on the use of these photos.

- The 1930 photograph of Hugh Walpole is in the collection of the Library of Congress Prints and Photographs Division. It is in the public domain because its copyright has expired.

- The portrait of Richard Burbage by an unknown painter is in the public domain because its copyright has expired.

- The 1948 panel from *The Phantom* comic strip written by Lee Falk and illustrated by Wilson McCoy is covered by copyright, but its use here is covered by U. S. fair use laws because it illustrates an educational article about the entity it represents, is used as the primary visual identification of the topic, is of low resolution and not suitable for the publication of counterfeit goods, is not used in such a way as to suggest to a reader that the use is authorized, and is not replaceable with an uncopyrighted image of comparable educational value.

- The photograph of Clarence Darrow is from the New York Public Library's Digital Library. It is in the public domain because its copyright is expired.

- The photograph of Susan B. Anthony was taken by Frances Benjamin Johnston, and is in the collection of the Library of Congress Prints and Photographs Division. It is in the public domain because its copyright is expired.

- The photograph of the Heinkel He 178 jet fighter is by the United States Air Force and is in the public domain as a work of the U.S. federal government.

- The illustration of the month of March used on the back cover and in the interior is from the French Gothic illuminated manuscript *Les Très Riches Heures du duc de Berry* by the Limbourg Brothers, Jean Colombe, and an intermediate painter whose name is lost to history. It is in the public domain because its copyright has expired.

- The photograph of aquamarine has been released into the public domain.

- The photograph of daffodils is by Myrabella, and is licensed under the Creative Commons Attribution-Share Alike 3.0 Unported license.

- The 1917 Women's Suffrage demonstration comes from the Library of Congress, Prints and Photographs Division, LC-USZ62-31799 DLC, and is in the public domain because its copyright has expired.

- The 50-year perpetual calendar photograph is in the public domain.